WORLD IN VIEW
ITALY
Barbara Walsh Angelillo

M
MACMILLAN

First published 1990

Published by
Macmillan Children's Books
A division of
MACMILLAN PUBLISHERS LTD
Houndmills, Basingstoke, Hampshire RG21 2XS
and London
Companies and representatives
throughout the world

Designed by Julian Holland Publishing Ltd
Additional picture research by Jennifer Johnson

Printed in Hong Kong

British Library Cataloguing in Publication Data
Angelillo, Barbara Walsh
  Italy.
  1. Italy
  I. Title II. Series
  945.092'8

ISBN 0-333-49332-X

Photographic credits:
Cover: Spectrum, title page: Rocco Spagnolo, 5, 9 Robert Harding Picture Library, 10, 21, 16, 17, 19 Rocco Spagnolo, 20 Paul Van Riel/Robert Harding Picture Library, 24 J. Allan Cash, 28, 29 Rocco Spagnolo, 31 Topham Picture Library, 34 Popperfoto, 37 Hutchinson Picture Library, 41, 42 Rocco Spagnolo, 43 Robert Harding Picture Library, 45, 47 Rocco Spagnolo, 49 Robert Harding Picture Library, 51 Rocco Spagnolo, 53 Robert Harding Picture Library, 55 Rocco Spagnolo, 56 Tophams Picture Library, 58 Rocco Spagnolo, 62 Robert Harding Picture Library, 63, 65, 68 Rocco Spagnolo, 69 M. Sinclair, 70, 71, 73 Rocco Spagnolo, 75, 76, 78, J. Allan Cash, 81 Robert Harding Picture Library, 83 Rocco Spagnolo, 84 J. Sturges, 85 Jennifer Johnson, 87, 89, 90 Rocco Spagnolo, 91 D. A. Lind/Antony Blake Photo Library, 92 Rocco Spagnolo.

Cover: *San Salute, Venice*
Title page: *horse drawn* caretto, *Sicily*

Contents

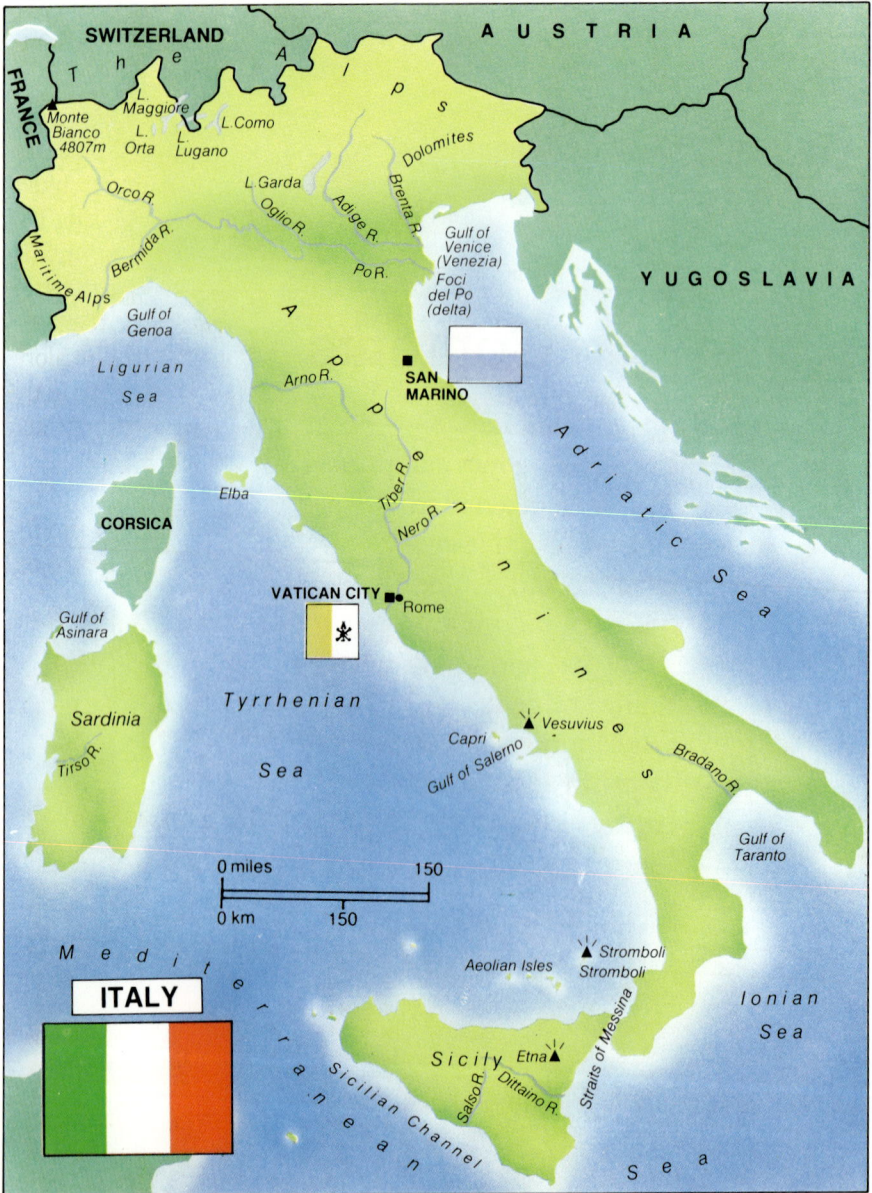

SWITZERLAND

A U S T R I A

FRANCE

T h e A l p s

Monte Bianco 4807m

L. Maggiore

L. Orta

L. Lugano

L. Como

YUGOSLAVIA

Orco R.

L. Garda

Dolomites

Oglio R.

Adige R.

Brenta R.

Maritime Alps

Bermida R.

Po R.

Gulf of Venice (Venezia)

Foci del Po (delta)

Gulf of Genoa

A
P

Arno R.

■ **SAN MARINO**

L i g u r i a n

S e a

P

e

Elba

Tiber R.

n

CORSICA

Nero R.

A d r i a t i c   S e a

VATICAN CITY ■

✳

● *Rome*

Gulf of Asinara

T y r r h e n i a n

n

Sardinia

S e a

Capri

▲ *Vesuvius*

e

Bradano R.

Tirso R.

Gulf of Salerno

s

Gulf of Taranto

0 miles   150

0 km   150

M e d i

t e

Aeolian Isles

☀ *Stromboli*
Stromboli

I o n i a n

S e a

ITALY

r

r

a

n

Sicilian Channel

Sicily

Salso R.

Dittaino R.

☀ *Etna* ▲

Straits of Messina

e a n

S e a

1

Introducing Italy

Italy is located in southern Europe. It is a long and narrow piece of land that extends into the central Mediterranean Sea. On a map Italy looks like a high-heeled boot with a wide cuff at the top. The cuff of the boot is formed by the high mountains called the Alps. The Alps make a barrier across the north of the country and separate Italy from the rest of Europe. Italy's only land borders lie along the Alps and divide the country from France in the west, Switzerland and Austria in the north and Yugoslavia in the east.

The leg of the boot is surrounded by parts of the Mediterranean Sea called the Ligurian Sea and the Tyrrhenian Sea to the west, the Adriatic Sea to the

The largest island in the Mediterranean, Sicily, has hot, dry summers and warm winters, with frequent dry spells. Farmers plant prickly pears in a row to form thick, spiny fences. They can grow as tall as trees in Sicily.

REGIONS OF ITALY

A map of Italy showing its regions and major cities, bordered by Switzerland, Austria, and Yugoslavia. Labelled regions include VALLE D'AOSTA, PIEMONTE, LOMBARDIE (LOMBARDY), TRENTINO-ALTO ADIGE, FRIULI-VENEZIA GIULIA, VENETO, LIGURIA, EMILIA ROMAGNA, TOSCANA (TUSCANY), MARCHE, UMBRIA, LAZIO, ABRUZZO, MOLISE, CAMPANIA, BASILICATA, APULIA, CALABRIA, SARDEGNA (SARDINIA), and SICILIA (SICILY). Bodies of water shown include the Ligurian Sea, Tyrrhenian Sea, Adriatic Sea, Ionian Sea, Mediterranean Sea, and Sicilian Channel. Cities labelled include Aosta, Torino (Turin), Milano (Milan), Bolzano, Trento, Verona, Cremona, Padova (Padua), Venezia (Venice), Trieste, Parma, Modena, Reggio nell' Emilia, Ferrara, Bologna, Genova (Genoa), San Remo, La Spezia, Viareggio, Pisa, Livorno, Firenze (Florence), Ravenna, Rimini, Ancona, Perugia, Pescara, ROMA (Rome), Foggia, Bari, Altamura, Napoli (Naples), Salerno, Brindisi, Taranto, Sassari, Cagliari, Cosenza, Palermo, Marsala, Messina, Reggio, Gela, Syracusa (Syracuse), and on Corsica and Sardegna.

0 miles 150
0 km 150

Italy's flag has three vertical stripes of red, white and green. From 1861 to 1946 the coat of arms of the Savoy kings appeared at the centre of the flag. It was removed when Italy became a republic.

east and the Ionian Sea to the south. The toe of the boot points toward Africa. On a map it looks as if the boot is kicking a football. That ball is the island of Sicily. Sicily and another island, Sardinia, are part of Italy, and they are the largest islands in the Mediterranean. The country includes many smaller offshore islands such as Capri and Elba, where the French emperor Napoleon spent a year in exile. The islands of Pantelleria and Lampedusa are located south-east of Sicily. Although they are closer to Africa than to Sicily, they are still part of Italy.

States and regions
Italy is more than 1000 kilometres (620 miles) long from top to toe. The cuff of the boot measures about 560 kilometres (350 miles) at its widest point in the north, but the leg of the boot is never more than 240 kilometres (150 miles) wide. The country has a total area of 301 225 square kilometres (116 300 square miles). It is about 1.2 times the size of the United Kingdom and about as large as the state of Arizona. Two tiny independent states exist within Italy's borders: San Marino in east-central Italy and the Vatican, inside the city of Rome. San Marino, which claims to be Europe's oldest republic, is governed by the people's elected representatives. It is not much larger than

The lira is the unit of currency in Italy, but one lira is worthless today, as value is calculated in hundreds, thousands and even millions of lire. An ice-cream cone costs about 1000 lire. A worker in the Fiat automobile factory earns more than a million lire each month, and the car he works on may cost as much as 20 million lire. Italians use coins worth from 10 to 500 lire and banknotes worth from 1000 to 100 000 lire. All those zeros make it difficult to keep accounts. The government is working on a scheme to revalue the currency, chopping off three zeros. Today's 1000 lire would become one lira.

the beautiful postage stamp for which it is famous, occupying only 61 square kilometres (24 square miles). Vatican City, where the pope lives, is even smaller than San Marino. It occupies just 0.44 square kilometres (0.17 square miles).

Italy is divided into 20 regions. Many regions existed long before Italy was united into a single state in 1861. Some regions can trace their history back thousands of years to when they were Roman provinces. Others established their borders when they were city-states or duchies, states ruled by a duke. The regions can be grouped in three main geographical areas. Northern Italy is made up of Liguria, Piedmont, Valle d'Aosta, Lombardy, Venetia, Trentino-Alto Adige and Friuli-Venezia Giulia. Central Italy includes the regions of Emilia-Romagna, Tuscany, Umbria, Latium and the Marches. Southern Italy is composed of the regions of Campania, Abruzzo, Molise, Basilicata, Calabria, Apulia, Sicily and Sardinia. Italians speak of only two divisions when they refer to the richer, industrialized north and the poorer, undeveloped south. They consider the dividing line to be the border between Latium and Campania.

Mountains and volcanoes

Most of the southern slopes of the Alps are located within Italy's borders. Alpine passes have been a gateway to Italy from the north since early times. These sharp peaks are characteristic of the section of the Alps known as the Dolomites. In the far distance is Marmolada, 3342 metres (10 965 feet), the highest mountain in the Dolomites.

Mountains or hills cover more than 75 per cent of Italy. The Alps lie across the northernmost part of the country. The highest peak in Italy is Monte Bianco, called Mont Blanc in France, in the Alps. It stands on the border with France and, at 3810 metres (15 780 feet) above sea level, it is also the highest mountain in Europe. A lower mountain system, called the Apennines, extends the length of the mainland and continues into Sicily. Mount Corno in the Abruzzo region is the highest mountain in the Apennines. It is also known as the

Scientists keep constant watch over Italy's active volcanoes, taking their temperatures and measuring their tremors so that they can warn of a coming eruption. There are many extinct volcanoes in Italy, too. Some of their craters form the beds of lakes.

Gran Sasso and rises 2910 metres (9580 feet) above sea level.

Some of the mountains in south-west Italy are active volcanoes. Mount Vesuvius, near Naples, sent a volcanic surge of molten rock and burning gas raining down on to the ancient Roman cities of Pompeii and Herculaneum in AD79. The eruption then buried the cities under a thick layer of red-hot ash and lava that preserved them until excavations began 1600 years later. Vesuvius last erupted in 1944. Mount Etna in Sicily is Europe's tallest active volcano. It is about 3300 metres (10 800 feet) high and a cap of snow covers its summit for most of the year. Mount Etna has had major eruptions as recently as 1983 and 1985. Stromboli and Vulcano, named after Vulcanus the

Roman god of fire, are smaller volcanoes located in the Aeolian Islands off Sicily.

People live in villages on the lower slopes of the volcanoes where they grow crops in the fertile volcanic soil. When the volcanoes are not active, tourists climb up the slopes to see the black wastelands of lava and volcanic ash near the craters.

Earthquakes

Deep below the surface of the Earth under Italy and the Mediterranean area, the massive curved plates that carry the continents of Europe and Africa move slowly and sometimes bump into each other. When this happens their edges shift and break. The movement of these shifting masses of rock sends out shock waves that cause earthquakes on the Earth's surface. Most of Italy is subject to earthquakes. The worst earthquake in Italy's history destroyed the Sicilian city of Messina in 1908, killing more than 70 000 people. In recent years, disastrous earthquakes struck the Friuli-Venezia Giulia region in 1976 and Campania in 1980. Thousands of people were killed and many towns were severely damaged.

Rivers and the climate

The longest and most important river in Italy is the Po River. It rises in the western Alps and flows across northern Italy to empty into the Adriatic Sea on the east. The Po is 650 kilometres (400 miles) long. It flows through a broad, fertile plain that stretches across northern Italy, covering slightly more than 16 per cent of the country's surface area. The Po Plain is the only large lowland in Italy and it is the country's major farming area. Second to the Po River in length are the Adige River in north-eastern Italy and the Tiber River, which flows through Rome in central Italy. Each is about 400 kilometres (250 miles) long. Mountainous countryside has encouraged the formation of several large lakes. Most of these are found in the north.

Italy has about 8000 kilometres (5000 miles) of coastline, ranging from broad sandy beaches to steep cliffs. Some towns like Positano cling to the cliffs above small bays. For a seaside holiday, many Italian and European tourists go to the shores of the Adriatic around Rimini, or to the coasts near Genoa or Pisa.

Italy has a generally mild climate but its length gives it marked contrasts between the northern and southern parts of the country. In Italy's coastal areas, summers may be long and hot but are cooled by breezes from the sea. Winters in these areas are short and mild. Summers can be very hot and humid in the lowlands of the interior but they are cool in the hills and mountains. Northern Italy has cold, wet winters and there are heavy snowfalls in the Alps and Apennines. The lowlands along the Po River are often blanketed with fog. The lakes are known for their mild climate throughout the year. The large northern lakes are sheltered from cold winds by the Alps. Although the winter season brings bitter cold to the mountains of the southern Apennines, the coasts and lowlands of southern Italy usually have warm, sunny winters.

The average maximum temperature in Milan in January is 4°C (40°F) and 29°C (84°F) in July while to the south Rome's temperature in January is 12°C (54°F) and 31°C (88°F) in July. The Italian mainland is exposed to a strong wind called the Sirocco. A hot and dry wind from the North African desert, the Sirocco picks up moisture as it crosses the Mediterranean and blows over southern Italy. It deposits a fine veil of reddish desert dust. Many areas of southern Italy get little rain and frequently suffer from drought.

Plants and animals
Evergreen forests grow on the slopes of the Alps and Apennines. Groves of chestnut, beech, oak, pine and olive trees cover the hillsides. In the mild climate of the coastal plains and Alpine lakes,

palm trees, oleanders and other Mediterranean plants grow. Cypress and umbrella pines are typical of central Italy and prickly pears, agave and eucalyptus grow in the more arid south.

Deer, wild pigs, foxes, hare and small forest animals live in the woodlands. Bear, wolves and ibex, or mountain goats, are rare but can still be found in some mountainous zones. Although eagles are becoming rare, falcons can frequently be seen soaring over fields and pastures in search of prey. In the sea, tuna, swordfish and dolphins can be found, and sardines, anchovies, cuttlefish and squid are plentiful.

There are five national parks and many nature reserves in Italy. The National Park of Stelvio in the Alps is the largest. It takes in portions of the mountainous zones of Lombardy and Trentino-Alto Adige. The Gran Paradiso Park in the western Alps includes parts of Piedmont and Valle d'Aosta. Chamois, a goatlike antelope, and ibex can be seen among the rocky crags of the Gran Paradiso, where many rare alpine plants grow. In central Italy, the National Park of Abruzzo is one of the few places in western Europe where the European bear can still be found. The Abruzzo Park extends into the neighbouring regions of Latium and Molise. The National Park of Circeo stands out on a mountainous headland on the coast of Latium. It shelters some ancient Roman ruins hidden among the low trees of the Mediterranean scrub. The National Park of Calabria includes some of the region's most isolated mountain areas. Near Oristano in Sardinia, flocks of flamingoes can be seen in early autumn in the nature reserve of San Vero Milis.

2 Emperors, popes and princes

For thousands of years many different groups of foreign settlers have been attracted to Italy. In ancient times many had migrated from northern lands in central Europe. Others were Mediterranean peoples who came to trade or establish colonies. Italy's geographical position at the centre of the Mediterranean made it a crossroads of the ancient world.

Most of the people who lived in Italy were farmers or shepherds. Each group had its own territory and spoke a different language. The Umbrians, for example, lived in a region of central Italy known as Umbria, and the Siculi people lived on the island of Sicily. Many place names in Italy recall the names of the people who lived there thousands of years ago.

The Etruscans

About 2800 years ago a group of people called the Etruscans ruled over a territory in central Italy known as Etruria, now called Tuscany. Some historians think that the Etruscans came by sea from the Middle East more than 3000 years ago. The Etruscans are important because they had a great influence on the ancient Romans. The Etruscans were skilled in crafts, especially metalworking, and they traded with other peoples in the Mediterranean area. They lived in strong, walled cities built on hilltops so that they could defend themselves easily from local tribes who

Most of what we know about the Etruscans has been learned from their tombs, which they decorated with colourful paintings of daily life and figures made from terracotta, such as these winged horses. They also filled the tombs with household objects in terracotta.

envied their riches. Etruscan temples were made of stone and wood with statues and colourful decorations in baked clay or terracotta. The wall paintings that decorate their tombs show that Etruscans liked feasts, games, music and dancing. Fine gold and ivory ornaments, beautiful vases imported from ancient Greece and bronze utensils have also been found in Etruscan tombs.

The founding of Rome
While the Etruscans lived and prospered in Etruria, the Latin people and their neighbours, the Sabines, shared a territory to the south along the Tiber River. Less advanced than the Etruscans, the Latins and Sabines lived in mud huts in small villages on seven low hills near the

river's banks. There they tended farms and livestock. In the eighth century BC, these villages were joined together to form a single, larger settlement called Rome. A legend says that Rome was founded in 753BC by Romulus and Remus, twin brothers who were abandoned as babies and were raised by a she-wolf. According to the legend Rome was named after Romulus. The Latin people who lived in Rome gave their name to the region of Latium and to the Latin language.

At about the same time as Rome was being founded, colonists from Greece settled along the coasts of southern Italy and Sicily. Their colonies grew to become fine cities with large temples and

Almost 3000 years ago Greeks settled in southern Italy. Their early settlements grew into wealthy cities, finer than those in Greece itself. Syracuse in Sicily was one of the most prosperous and beautiful of these cities. This Greek amphitheatre in Syracuse is still being used today as a theatre.

outdoor theatres called amphitheatres. The Greek language and culture spread through southern Italy.

In the sixth century BC the Etruscans reached a peak of wealth and power. They extended their rule northwards from Etruria into the plain of the Po River. They seized control of Rome and pushed southwards into Campania. Rome grew in size and importance under the Etruscan kings, but the Romans wanted to be independent. About 500BC they rebelled against the Etruscans and made Rome a republic. It was governed by two elected leaders called consuls. They were advised by a senate made up of patricians, who were wealthy aristocrats. At first, the common citizens, called *plebs* or plebeians, had little to say about how Rome was governed. However, they gradually forced the patricians to grant them more rights. An assembly of citizens was formed to participate in governing the republic.

The early Romans gained control over the many different groups of people in Italy by making war

A republic is a form of government in which power to rule the country or the state is given to the people and the representatives they have elected to run the country. A republic does not have a king as a ruler. Instead, the people vote to elect their representatives.
The Roman republic consisted of two leaders or consuls, the senate and popular assemblies. Power was in the hands of the patricians, or wealthy aristocrats, until the plebeians, or common people, after two centuries of struggle, gained places in all state offices.

The Colosseum is one of the most impressive of all the Roman remains. It was four storeys high and could seat 47 000 people. It was used for fights between gladiators or wild beasts. The floor of the arena, which has since collapsed revealing the rooms beneath, could also be flooded for mock naval battles.

on their neighbours or by forming alliances with them. They imposed their own system of government and Roman law on the people they conquered, such as the Etruscans in Tuscany and the Greek colonies in southern Italy. By the third century BC, the entire Italian peninsula and Sicily were under Roman rule.

The Romans were skilled engineers and architects. They had learned much about building from the Etruscans, who were the first people in the western world to use the arch. The Romans developed new uses for the arch, employing it in aqueducts, which carried water, and in bridges and domes. The Romans also built a network of good roads which helped them win military success.

19

The Pantheon in Rome is a fine example of classical architecture. It was built by the Emperor Hadrian about AD120 to serve as a temple to all the gods. In Greek, pan *means 'all' and* theos *means 'god'. Like other important Roman buildings, it was decorated inside and out with precious marble and gilded bronze.*

The Punic Wars

Once it had gained control of Italy, Rome sent its armies to conquer the rest of the ancient world. One victory led to another and Rome became the chief land power in the Mediterranean area. However, power on the sea was held by Carthage, an ancient city-state on the coast of North Africa. Carthage was founded by the Phoenicians, a seafaring people from the Middle East. Carthaginian warships were the strongest and fastest in the Mediterranean. In 264BC, Rome challenged Carthage's mastery of the sea in the first of three wars known as the Punic Wars. About 40 years later during the Second Punic War, Hannibal, a Carthaginian general, led 60 000 men and dozens of elephants across the Alps in an attempt to invade Italy. After more than 100 years, Rome finally destroyed Carthage in the Third Punic War. During the first century BC Rome was torn by political conflict and civil war. In order to prevent chaos, Julius Caesar, a great military commander and statesman took power. Some Romans feared that Caesar would have himself crowned as king, bringing about the end of the declining republic. Caesar was assassinated in 44BC, but the republic was too weak to survive much longer. In 27BC, Caesar's nephew and heir, Octavian, won the struggle for power. He was proclaimed Rome's first emperor and was given the name of Augustus.

The Roman empire

The reign of Augustus marked the beginning of a period of peace that lasted for 200 years. During this period the Roman empire reached its greatest extent. It stretched from the Middle East to Spain in the west and from the Sahara in North Africa northwards as far as Britain. Even the far corners of the empire were linked with Rome by fine roads. Roman engineers built bridges and aqueducts in the provinces. The ruins of Roman cities can still be seen today in the deserts of North Africa. In the second century AD Emperor Hadrian ordered his engineers to build a defence wall more than 110 kilometres (70 miles) long across the narrowest part of the island of Great

Britain. Hadrian's Wall was two metres (six feet) high and 2.5 metres (eight feet) thick, and parts of it still stand. Roman citizenship was granted to all free men in the empire, and Roman laws were administered in the courts. Trade and the arts flourished.

More than a million people lived in the city of Rome at the time of the empire. Rome had paved streets, a sewer system, running water supplied by aqueducts, a fire service and a police force. The wealthy lived in homes with airy courtyards and walled gardens. Ordinary citizens lived in poorer houses or in blocks of flats several storeys high. Roman buildings were made of concrete, which the Romans invented. Walls were faced with brick and then covered with stucco, a hard surfacing material, which was painted. The most important buildings were often faced with marble. The emperors built magnificent arenas, theatres, temples and baths to glorify themselves and to win the people's favour. In the huge arena called the Colosseum more than 50 000 people could watch the cruel fights of the gladiators. Thousands of wild beasts were brought to Rome from provinces in Africa and the Middle East to be killed in the Colosseum.

The decline of the Roman empire
At the height of Rome's power, rich Romans amused themselves with lavish feasts. The poor were provided with free food and entertainment at arenas and circuses, or hippodromes, to keep them from rebelling. As the empire expanded into the Mediterranean and western Europe, it became too large and too costly to maintain. Not even

heavy taxes could provide enough money to guard the distant borders, feed the people and maintain the luxurious standard of living that the Romans demanded. Gradually, the Romans lost their respect for duty, for the family, for the state and for their gods.

In the third century, the empire was divided into two parts with a ruler in both east and west. In 330 Emperor Constantine reunited the empire but moved the capital away from Rome to the city of Byzantium, in what is now Turkey. He renamed the city Constantinople. The empire grew weaker and Italy was invaded by groups of people known as the Vandals and Goths, who came from lands that are part of Germany, Hungary and the USSR today. The last Roman emperor was overthrown by the invaders in 476.

When the Roman empire fell, Italy's unity was shattered. Foreign rulers struggled to gain control over parts of the peninsula. The Arabs conquered Sicily in the ninth century, and they were conquered in turn by the Normans, fair-haired princes from northern France. Charlemagne, a

The Holy Roman Empire dates from 800 when Charlemagne was crowned Holy Roman Emperor by Pope Leo III. The name itself was used in 1254 to refer to the European lands ruled by a series of German kings, including Otto II. At the height of its power, the empire included modern Germany, Austria, western Czechoslovakia, Switzerland, eastern France, the Netherlands and much of Italy. The empire finally ended in 1806 and so did the use of the imperial title.

German king, formed an alliance with the powerful leader of the Christian Church. This leader, called the pope, ruled in Rome. Together Charlemagne and the pope created the Holy Roman Empire, and the pope crowned Charlemagne emperor in 800. The Holy Roman Empire reached its greatest extent and power shortly after Charlemagne's coronation. Eventually, however, popes and emperors became rivals for power in Italy. The people took sides in the struggle and local princes fought for one side or the other. For centuries afterwards, Italy remained divided into small states ruled by princes.

The rise of the city-states

From the tenth to the fifteenth century, a number of strong and independent city-states emerged in northern and central Italy, each with its own form of government. Some had their own army or navy. City-states such as Milan, Mantua and Genoa became great duchies. The most important city-states were Venice and Florence. Venice was founded on islands near the mouth of the Adige River by refugees from the invasions. The city grew rich by trading in silks, spices, perfumes and jewels from the Orient. Florence, a prosperous centre of commerce and banking, was ruled by the wealthy Medici family. Profitable trade brought well-being to the people and put Italy in contact with other parts of the world. Italian merchants, such as Marco Polo who came from Venice, travelled throughout Europe and Asia. Not even outbreaks of plague, called the Black Death, in the fourteenth century affected general prosperity.

The tall tower of Palazzo Vecchio has been part of Florence's skyline since it was built, as the city hall, in 1301. A stone lion, the city's symbol, stands in front of the palace. The buildings by the flower market are fine examples of later Renaissance architecture. One is the Uffizi Gallery which houses one of the finest art collections in the world.

The Renaissance

By the fourteenth and fifteenth centuries, a surge of cultural energy was spreading through Italy. It was called the Renaissance, which means 'rebirth'. There was a renewed interest in the artistic works and writings of the ancient Greeks and Romans. Under the wealthy Medici dukes,

Florence became a great centre of art and learning. The Medicis encouraged scholars, poets, craftsmen and artists and paid them for their work. During the long rule of the Medicis, the architect Brunelleschi designed the revolutionary dome of Florence's cathedral. It was the first great dome to be raised since that of the Pantheon in Rome. Many talented artists, such as Michelangelo and Leonardo da Vinci, worked for the Medicis. The scientist Galileo served as mathematician and astronomer in the Medici court. Florence's artists, architects and craftsmen were called to work for other rulers in Italy and Europe. Michelangelo was summoned to Rome by the popes while Leonardo da Vinci invented amazing devices for the duke of Milan and later worked for the king of France.

The Renaissance spread throughout Europe in the fifteenth and sixteenth centuries. It changed the way people thought about the world they lived in, by pointing out the possibilities of human intelligence. It changed the appearance of many cities as builders opened up large squares and put up great palaces and churches. The Renaissance was one of the greatest cultural movements the world has ever known.

3   The birth of a nation

The Renaissance gave Italy beautiful buildings and magnificent works of art, but it was not a peaceful period. Constant fighting between popes, emperors and local princes kept the country divided into rival states. Meanwhile, stronger and united nations such as France, Spain and Austria gained control over parts of Italy. The people of Italy were taxed heavily under foreign rule and their land was a battleground for the soldiers of other countries. A small number of wealthy lords and landowners lived in great luxury while most of the people suffered in poverty and dependence. The Austrians who ruled northern Italy were harsh masters. In the south, the Bourbons, who belonged to a branch of Spain's royal family, gave the people little freedom.

Many Italians welcomed the invasion of Italy by the French general Napoleon Bonaparte at the end of the eighteenth century. The Italians hoped that French rule would be less harsh than that of the Austrians or Bourbons. Between 1796 and 1814, the French dominated the entire Italian peninsula. They built new roads and gave Italy new laws. Napoleon succeeded in unifying the separate states of Italy for the first time since the Roman empire. However, Napoleon was defeated by other European powers and most Italian states were returned to their former rulers.

The Risorgimento

The Italians' hatred of foreign domination grew as Italy was divided again into seven states.

During the reign of the Bourbon kings in the eighteenth century, Naples was one of Europe's most important cities. The Bourbon palace at Caserta was modelled on the French royal palace at Versailles. Caserta has 1200 rooms, many of which were richly decorated and furnished.

Lombardy-Venetia, Tuscany, Parma and Modena were all ruled by Austria; the Kingdom of the Two Sicilies was ruled by the Bourbons and the Papal States by the pope. The Kingdom of Sardinia-Piedmont was the only independent state and was ready to guide the rest of Italy on the path to unity. In the early nineteenth century many Italians joined in a movement called the Risorgimento, which aimed to drive out foreign rulers and unify Italy into one free nation. Not all of the patriots who took part in the Risorgimento agreed on how to do this. A well-known writer and thinker, Giuseppe Mazzini, called for a revolution that would lead to the formation of a republic. His method was opposed by the clever diplomat Camillo di Cavour, who served as prime minister

Garibaldi and the Red Shirts
The military hero of the Risorgimento was
Giuseppe Garibaldi, who commanded a
brigade of volunteer soldiers in bright red shirts.
In 1860, Garibaldi and the 'Red Shirts' won
fame as bold fighters for the cause of freedom
in Italy when they freed Sicily at the battle of
Calatafimi and then went on to liberate the
southern mainland. Nine million more Italians
were freed from the hated Bourbon kings and
brought under the rule of the Piedmontese king
Victor Emmanuel II.

*Guiseppe Garibaldi,
Italy's national hero, was
the son of a fisherman. He
became a daring military
leader, fighting in wars of
liberation not only in Italy
but also in South America.
His wife Anita fought by
his side against the
Austrians who occupied
Italy. Garibaldi died, aged
75, in his cottage on the
island of Patrera, off
Sardinia.*

to Victor Emmanuel II, king of Sardinia-Piedmont. Cavour planned and carried out the political moves that welded a number of small Italian states into one nation.

A new nation

By 1861, most of Italy was united and Victor Emmanuel II was proclaimed king of the new nation. Another victory drove the Austrian occupation troops out of Venice in 1866. The Papal State of Rome did not become part of the new country, however, because Pope Pius IX opposed unification. In 1870, when Italian troops forced their way into Rome, the pope withdrew behind the walls of the Vatican. He remained free to exercise his authority as head of the Church, but could only rule over the Vatican. It was not until 1929 that the Vatican was recognized as an independent state, as it is today.

The making of the new nation did not end Italy's problems, however. It was deeply in debt and the people were still divided by regional differences in dialect and customs. They could not agree on how the country should be governed. Despite many difficulties, Italy built schools and railways. It established an army and a navy. Industrial expansion brought prosperity to northern Italy, but the south remained poor and undeveloped. Between 1870 and 1914, more than 10 million people emigrated from Italy, setting out for foreign countries in search of a better life.

Two World Wars

In 1915, Italy entered the First World War (1914-1918) to fight on the side of Britain and France against Austria. After the war, the Italian economy plunged into a depression and people began to leave the country again in search of jobs. The people who stayed protested against hard times by going on strike and rioting in the streets. Benito Mussolini, who became leader of the Fascist party that seized power in 1922, promised to restore order to the nation. Instead the Fascists silenced all other political parties, using violence and terror to crush all opposition. Although the king was still on the throne, Mussolini was an absolute dictator. He was called *Il Duce* (The leader). Mussolini dreamed of creating another Roman empire. He built up Italy's army and navy and conquered the African country of Ethiopia. In 1936, Mussolini joined in an alliance with Adolf Hitler, the Nazi leader of Germany. Four years

Founder of the Fascist party in 1921, Benito Mussolini was a schoolteacher and worked as a journalist before entering politics and becoming dictator. His alliance with Hitler, seen here with Mussolini, and the resulting disastrous warmongering, made him very unpopular with most Italians.

later, Italy entered the Second World War (1940-1945) on the side of Germany, fighting against the Allied Forces of Britain, the United States and other countries.

The Italians had neither the military strength nor the will to fight a large-scale war that most of them did not want. After the Allies invaded Sicily in 1943, the Italians forced Mussolini to resign. A few months later, Italy surrendered to the Allies and declared war on its former ally, Germany. German troops still controlled much of Italy. The war continued for two years as the Allies slowly drove the German army northwards. Fortunately, both sides kept a promise to preserve Rome from war damage. The long and bitter struggle ended in 1945. Bombs and artillery had destroyed factories, roads, railway lines and entire towns. Battles had wrecked the countryside. The people did not have enough to eat and many had lost their homes and their jobs.

Italy's post-war boom

Once again Italy was faced with the huge problems of recovering from a major war. Through the European Recovery Programme, the Allies supplied aid to help Italy rebuild its industry and agriculture. In 1946, the Italian people voted to replace the monarchy with a democratic republic. The king went into exile and a new constitution, setting out the basic rules and principles by which the nation would be governed, was written. The constitution went into effect on 1 January 1948.

During the 1950s, industrial recovery led to a giant economic boom. Prosperity gradually changed the way many Italians lived. For the first time workers' families could afford to own their own homes, cars and television sets. More than three million people from southern Italy were attracted by factory and construction jobs in Turin, Milan and other cities in the north. At the same time, about eight million more Italians emigrated to other European countries to find work. Half of them eventually returned to Italy, but half settled permanently in countries such as Switzerland, West Germany and the United Kingdom. In Italy the gap between the prosperous north and the poor south widened, as business managers were reluctant to invest money in a region with a declining workforce and a poor network of roads. In 1949, Italy became a member of the North Atlantic Treaty Organization (NATO), a defensive alliance of friendly nations, and in 1955, the country was admitted to the United Nations. Together with five other European nations, Belgium, France, Luxembourg, the Netherlands and West Germany, it was a founding member of the European Community (EC), also called the Common Market.

The constitution and government

Italy's system of government consists of a parliament made up of two houses, the Chamber of Deputies and the Senate. Both houses must approve laws. Deputies are elected for five-year terms. Senators serve six-year terms. Both houses elect the president of Italy for a seven-year term. The president is the head of state. He names a prime minister who is head of the government. The prime minister, called the president of the

The Corazzieri, guard of honour for the president of Italy, wear showy uniforms and are all about two metres (more than six feet) tall. The official residence of the Italian president is the Quirinale palace in Rome, built by the popes in the sixteenth century as a summer home. It was to the Quirinale that Giovanni Goria came to be nominated as prime minister-designate in 1987 by the president, Francesco Cossiga.

Council, and his ministers, who are Council members, establish government policy.

All Italians over 18 vote for the members of the Chamber of Deputies. Voters over 21 elect the members of the Senate. About 80 per cent of the Italians who are eligible, vote in political elections. An even greater number of people vote in elections for regional, provincial and city governments.

During the Second World War, three main political parties emerged in Italy. They were the

Christian Democrats, the Communists and the Socialists. However, there are many more political parties today. At least nine parties usually present candidates for national elections. As a result, no single party is strong enough in parliament to ensure passage of proposed laws. In order to control a majority of the votes needed to pass the laws that the government proposes, the prime minister forms a coalition or combination of several parties that will support the government.

If the prime minister loses the support of the parties in the coalition, or if parliament will not give him a vote of confidence, the prime minister resigns. His government 'falls' and Italy's president names another prime minister who forms another government. There have been more than 45 changes of government since the republic was proclaimed on 2 June 1946. Governments in Italy last an average of 11 months. The government headed by Socialist Bettino Craxi, from 1983 to 1987, was the longest in the history of the republic.

4   Home life and leisure

Italy has a population of more than 57 million, slightly more than the United Kingdom. Like the United Kingdom, it is one of the most crowded countries in Europe. There are an average of 190 people per square kilometre (0.6 mile) in Italy, as compared with about 230 in the United Kingdom, 76 in Spain, 25 in the USA or two per square kilometre in Australia. From 1861, when Italy became one nation, the country's population increased steadily and rapidly for more than 100 years. Today, the number of births and number of deaths each year in Italy are almost equal. The growth of the population is slowing down.

Today, a large number, almost 75 per cent of the Italians, live in cities and towns in the country's lowlands. Before the Second World War, 50 per cent of the people lived on farms or in villages. Industrial expansion in north-western Italy after the war created jobs in the north that attracted millions of people from other parts of the country. Most of them came from the poorer, mainly agricultural south. About three million people live in Rome, Italy's capital and largest city. The area around Milan and Turin, two important industrial centres in the prosperous north, is thickly populated. The largest cities in southern Italy are Naples and Palermo, which are very overcrowded and rundown. Millions of Italians have emigrated and there are large Italian colonies in other European countries, as well as in the USA, Canada, South America and Australia.

In the centres of cities people often live in flats. The older buildings are often run down but many are brightened by small balcony gardens. In cities like Naples many of the older buildings have become slums.

Language

Italian is the official language of the nation. It is based on ancient Latin and on the language that was spoken in Florence during the thirteenth and fourteenth centuries. This was the language in which the poet Dante and others wrote the first Italian literary works, and it developed into the Italian language as it is spoken today. People speak Italian with accents that differ from one region to another. Some regions have dialects that are very different from Italian. Sardinia has its own language but the Sardinians also speak the Italian language. In north-western Italy near the French border, many people speak French. German is spoken in Alto Adige, which was part of Germany until 1918. Street signs and official documents in

Alto Adige are written in both Italian and German. Some people in the Dolomites and in the Friuli region speak a language called Ladin. Ladin can be traced back to the ancient Latin spoken by the soldiers of the Roman empire who settled in remote mountain valleys. Their descendants remained cut off from other people for many centuries and their language changed very little. In some small areas of southern Italy people speak Albanian or Greek. This was the language of their ancestors, who came to Italy as refugees hundreds of years ago when their homelands were invaded by Turkish armies.

How the Italians live
The Italians are usually friendly and outgoing. They are quick to smile and they generally don't hide their feelings when they are sad or angry. They are not timid about showing affection, especially for babies and children, whom they love.

Family life is very important to most Italians. In the past the typical Italian family was made up of many members, including grandparents, aunts, uncles and cousins. They all lived together and they all contributed in some way to the family's well-being, either by helping at home or by working to bring in money. Many businesses were owned and run by a single family. Today, traditional family groups can be found mainly on farms and in small towns. The typical family group lives in cities and large towns. It is made up of a mother and father and one or two children. Their relatives may live on the other side of the city or even in another part of the country. Family ties are still strong, however. Families keep in touch by telephone and have reunions whenever they can.

Where people live

In large cities and towns people live in flats. Sometimes the flats are in very old buildings on narrow streets in the oldest parts of town. In Rome, Milan and Turin, which grew rapidly after the Second World War, the beautiful old buildings in the heart of the city are surrounded by dreary neighbourhoods made up of blocks of flats built in the 1950s and 1960s. The newer suburbs on the edge of the cities are more attractive, with neat houses and parks. Many historic cities and towns such as Venice, Siena in Tuscany and Gubbio in Umbria look just the same today as they did hundreds of years ago.

A typical flat in Italy has a living-dining room, where there is usually a large table for family dinners on Sundays. The kitchen may have a small table for everyday meals. There may be two bedrooms and a bathroom. Many flats have balconies or small terraces filled with plants. About six out of 10 Italians own their own homes and some also own a holiday flat at the seaside or a house in the country. Most families have cars, television sets and a number of electric appliances. The standard of living of most people is higher than it was 30 years ago. Italy's post-war economic boom changed the way people live.

Work and play

Although agriculture is an important part of the Italian economy, the percentages of people employed in farming continued to fall in the 1980s. Nearly half of the Italian workforce is employed in the service sector. This includes jobs in government offices, banks, insurance companies, shops, hotels and restaurants. Unemployment is a serious problem in Italy today. More than half of the unemployed are young people looking for their first jobs. They were born during the so-called baby boom of the 1960s, when Italy's population increased rapidly. Not enough jobs are available for this age group, and many cannot find work. The problem is relieved for a short while when Italian boys over 18 are required to serve in a branch of the army or navy from 12 to 18 months. In most families women work at home, taking care of the children and doing the housework, shopping and cooking. However, in one out of three families both father and mother work.

In the cooler climate of northern Italy the work day lasts from morning until late afternoon. People take a short break for lunch at midday. They either bring their lunch from home or have a snack in a food shop. In central and southern Italy, most shops and many offices close in the middle of the day for two or three hours. People go home for lunch and may take a nap before returning to work. Children come home from school at about 1 pm and they usually do their homework after lunch. Then they have time to play or take lessons in music or sports.

The work day ends in the late afternoon or early evening. The family has their evening meal and may watch television. In their free time people enjoy strolling in the centre of town, where they

The passeggiata, *or promenade, is a social ritual that Italy shares with other Mediterranean countries. At a certain time of day, usually in the late afternoon, people gather to stroll up and down the town's main street. They greet their friends and chat about the day's events, and they may stop at a cafe for ice-cream or coffee.*

look at the shop windows and may stop at a cafe. In small towns and villages, men gather at local cafes where they play cards and talk about politics. People prefer watching films on television rather than going to the cinema.

Sports and holidays

Many Italians are soccer fans. On Sunday afternoon they watch soccer games on television or go to see the local team play. Games in the stadiums of Turin, Milan, Naples and Rome attract thousands of fans. People are very interested in soccer news and stories about highly-paid soccer players. The Italian national soccer team won the World Cup in 1982 and Italy will be host of the 1990 World Cup games.

Soccer is Italy's favourite sport, and Italian teams often win international cups. Soccer fans play a weekly betting game, Totip, which pays large sums of money to lucky winners. Totip is a lottery run by the state, which uses part of the money to build new sports centres for the public.

Skiing, tennis and cycling are also popular sports, both to watch and to practise. The Grand Tour of Italy is a cycling event that takes place each year along a course stretching from one end of the peninsula to the other. Motor-racing and sailing are also popular. Bowls, called *bocce,* is a favourite pastime and there are millions of

Carnivals

Lively carnivals are held just before Lent, the 40-day period before Easter. Carnival at Viareggio in Tuscany features a parade of giant floats. Many festivals recall historic events. The famous Palio is a breakneck race run in the main square of Siena in Tuscany. It recalls the rivalry between the city's various districts, and it is named after the palio, a banner that is awarded to the winner. The Palio takes place twice a year, on 2 July and 16 August. Most festivals in Italy end with a spectacular show of fireworks that fill the sky with noise and colour.

The people of Siena spend months preparing for the Palio, a horse race that lasts only two minutes. Festivities include a parade of people dressed in rich medieval costumes and exhibitions of flag-throwing.

licensed hunters in Italy but there is little game. Conservationists support laws that would limit or prohibit hunting.

Italians enjoy celebrating festivals. Most festivals are linked to religious events, such as Easter or Christmas or to the annual feast day of the local patron saint. Every saint has a feast day and every town has a patron saint. On the saint's feast there is usually a colourful procession, and there may be a special market, entertainment and sports events.

August is holiday month in Italy during which almost all the factories, offices and shops in large cities are closed. Most people leave the cities for a holiday by the sea or in the mountains.

5 Farming and fishing

Although over 75 per cent of Italy is hilly or mountainous, more than half of the land is cultivated. Soil and climate are so varied that crops and methods of farming are adapted to the local conditions. People make terraces on the steep hillsides in order to grow grapes and olives, which they must harvest by hand. More gentle slopes are well suited to larger vineyards. In the flat, fertile lowlands, farm machines make work easier and farmers can cultivate a variety of crops over large areas. Irrigation schemes and greenhouses make it possible to produce profitable crops on land that was once infertile.

Large numbers of farms throughout Italy cultivate grapes for wine. Italians produce, consume and export more wine than any other country. The best known wines come from Piedmont, Lombardy and Veneto in the north and from Tuscany in central Italy.

Farming land

Italy's best farming land is in the vast lowland that stretches on either side of the Po River, from Piedmont in the west to Emilia-Romagna in the east. Crops are produced on the narrow coastal plains bordering the Apennines, although many of the plains are marshy and have to be drained before they can be cultivated. A broad plain extends along the toe and heel of Italy's boot in the Apulia region.

Most of Italy's farms are between 5 and 100 hectares (12 and 240 acres) in size, and they are usually run by one family. Fewer people work on farms today. Many have moved to jobs in the cities. At harvest time farmers hire temporary workers to pick the crops. Young people who are unemployed may earn some money this way. In southern Italy, farmers hire migrant workers from North Africa for very low wages. Many farmers join associations called co-operatives, which provide advice on the best way to grow crops and which help process and market farm products.

Grapes and olives

Italy is one of the world's largest producers of wine and olive oil. Grapes are grown on more than half of the farms, and many farms are made up almost entirely of vineyards. The owners take great pride in making their own wine and they sell it in bottles with the name of the farm and the owner on the label. Experts say that some of these wines are among the best in the world. Other farmers may grow large quantities of grapes and take them to a co-operative to be made into wine. The co-operative puts its own label on the wine and

Olive trees

Olive trees are a typical feature of Italy's landscape. Their gnarled trunks and small, silvery leaves can be seen in the groves covering hillsides in Liguria, Tuscany and many other regions in central and southern Italy, including Sicily and Sardinia. An olive tree must be about 30 years old before it bears fruit, but it may continue to produce olives for hundreds of years. Olives are good to eat after they are cured in brine, or salted water. Most of the olives grown in Italy are crushed and made into olive oil. Italy is the second largest producer of olive oil in the world.

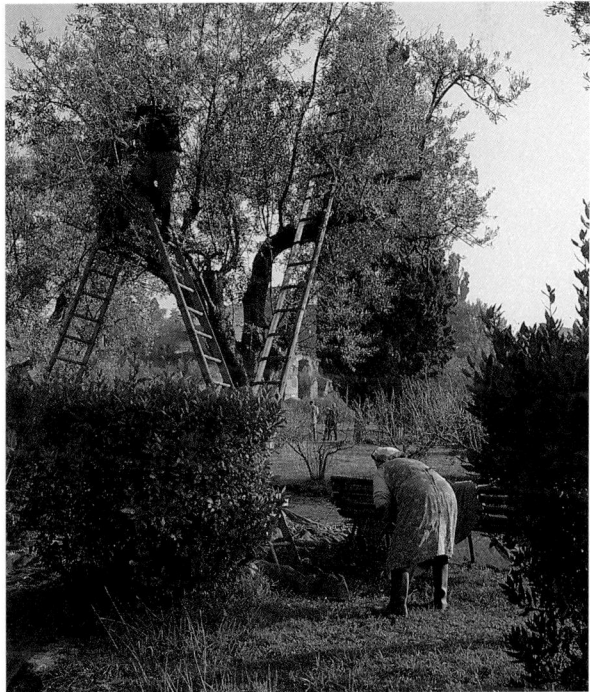

When olives are ready for picking, farmers spread coloured nets under the trees and beat the branches with poles. The olives fall on to the nets and can be gathered easily. An olive tree is shown on Italy's 100-lire coin as a symbol of peace.

sells it to dealers. The profits are divided among the members of the co-operative.

The most famous Italian wines come from northern and central Italy. Chianti wine is produced in Tuscany. It can be found on menus in Italian restaurants all over the world. However, Apulia in southern Italy produces more wine than any other region, with Sicily a close second. Apulia's sunny vineyards yield sweeter grapes that make wine with a higher alcoholic content. Most of the wine produced in the south is not bottled but is sent to wineries in the north where it is mixed with local wines to make them stronger.

Grapes and olives are crops well suited to Italy's hilly landscape, which also yields chestnuts and hazelnuts from wooded areas. Cork trees grow in Sardinia. Woodlands also produce mushrooms and truffles, particularly delicious mushrooms that grow hidden in the soil. Dogs are specially trained to sniff and dig them out.

Lowland crops
Other than grapes, Italy's chief crops are sugar beets, wheat, corn and tomatoes. All of these crops are grown on the vast Po plain. Rice and fruit are also grown in large quantities on the Po plain. The hard durum wheat that is used to make pasta is an important crop in Apulia, Sicily and Sardinia. The lowlands and coastal plains of Apulia, Sicily and Campania produce a variety of vegetables that are shipped to markets in northern Italy and in other countries. Italy's farms produce artichokes, onions and cauliflowers but tomatoes, potatoes and melons are the chief vegetable crops.

Italy is Europe's largest producer and exporter

of citrus fruits, such as oranges, tangerines, and lemons, most of which are grown in Sicily. Apples and pears are produced in the orchards of northern and central Italy and peaches are grown in Campania. In recent years, kiwi fruit have become an important fruit crop in central Italy.

By using greenhouses covered with transparent plastic, farmers in sunny southern Italy can produce several crops of vegetables every year. Today, it's possible to find plump bell peppers and shiny purple aubergines in Italian markets all year round. Growers using similar methods have made Italy a major producer of cut flowers and house plants.

Chemicals used in agriculture to fertilize the soil and to kill insects and weeds may cause environmental damage. These chemicals can soak

Tuscany's cowboys are called butteri. *They ride horses and carry long poles to prod the long horned white cattle typical of the region. They can be seen in the Meremma district, Tuscany's coastal plain. This was once a marshy area infested with malaria. Today, it has been drained and is fertile land suitable for farming and grazing.*

through the earth and pollute the vein of water from which towns and cities draw their drinking water. The pollution problem is becoming a serious one in many areas of Italy. Environmental protection groups are encouraging research into more natural ways to make crops grow.

Livestock and fishing

In Sardinia and Sicily large flocks of sheep are a common sight. There are almost four million sheep on the island of Sardinia alone. More than a million sheep graze on the poor grasslands of Sicily, and an equal number of sheep are raised in central Italy. Their milk is used to make cheese. In Sardinia, shepherds may spend a month or more in remote areas far from their villages. They carry a special kind of crisp bread called *carta da musica* (music paper) in their packs. It is made of flour and water. Baked in very thin sheets, it looks something like the parchment paper that church music was written on hundreds of years ago.

Large pig farms on the Po plain produce meat for the famous Italian ham called *prosciutto* and for many types of salami and sausage. Cattle are raised in northern Italy, but much of the meat sold in Italy has to be imported. On the coastal plain of the Maremma in Tuscany, herdsmen called *butteri* hold traditional contests that are similar to rodeos.

Although Italy has about 8000 kilometres (5000 miles) of coast, fishing is not as important as it once was. Many of the small fishing towns that dot the coast have become tourist towns. Pollution and overfishing result in smaller fishing catches. Not enough fish is caught to satisfy the demand for fresh fish at the market, so fresh and frozen fish

Although Italy is surrounded by water, the fishing industry is losing importance. Overfishing and pollution in the Mediterranean have resulted in smaller catches and low profits. Most of the fish caught by Italian fishermen come from the Adriatic.

must be bought from other nations. However, sardines, mackerel and anchovies are plentiful and tuna, swordfish, squid and octopus are caught in Italian waters too. The largest and most active fishing ports are located along the coast of the Adriatic Sea and in Sicily. The brackish water of the Po delta, where the river meets the sea, is ideal for raising eels and other types of fish. There are many fisheries in the area. Fishermen raise oysters, clams and other molluscs in the shallow waters of the Adriatic and in the Bay of Taranto.

6 Industry and trade

Although Italy is not rich in raw materials and mineral resources, it is one of the world's major industrial powers ranking close to the United Kingdom. Italy is a leading producer of manufactured goods. Italian industries import raw materials and transform them into products that are sold in Italy or exported to other countries.

The Italian flair for design contributes to the success of many products. Designers in Italy are expert in blending style and function even in everyday objects, from cars and washing machines to hi-tech lamps and furniture. Italy's principal natural resources are stone and marble, sulphur, mercury and natural gas. The country's chief industries produce chemicals, processed foods, textiles, motor vehicles, machines and mechanical parts.

Carrara marble
Marble is a very hard limestone that can be polished and is suitable for carving. Almost half of the marble used in the world comes from Italy, which also exports granite and stone. Fine white Carrara marble comes from huge quarries in the mountains between Genoa and Pisa. The ancient Romans quarried marble in these mountains 2000 years ago. Michelangelo used to join the workmen in the quarries, searching for perfect pieces of marble for his statues. There is so much marble in the mountains that it can be quarried for many more centuries.

High in the mountains near Carrara, between Genoa and Pisa, huge slabs of white marble are quarried. Much of Carrara's marble is exported. Italy also produces pumice, gypsum, potash and salt from native rocks.

Oil and gas

The country's most highly industrialized area is the north-west, close to the Alps where hydro-electric power is plentiful. However, hydro-electric power alone cannot satisfy the energy needs of Italian industry. Since Italy's fuel resources are limited, the country must import large amounts of oil and natural gas and some coal in order to run its power plants. Italy imports crude oil from the Middle East and Libya which is processed in large refineries in Sicily and in northern Italy. Giant pipelines carry natural gas to Italy from the Netherlands and the USSR. Another pipeline stretches from Algeria's gas fields in the Sahara and plunges under the Mediterranean Sea, surfacing in Sicily. It supplies gas to southern and central Italy. Today, oil and gas meet 75 per cent of Italy's energy requirements. Hydro-electric power furnishes the rest. Italy has a few nuclear power stations and more are planned, but many groups oppose their construction.

The industrial triangle

In the north-west, the cities of Turin, Milan and Genoa form an area called the industrial triangle, which includes many smaller cities and towns. Many of Italy's largest industries are located in this area. The Fiat company, whose motor works are in Turin, was founded almost 100 years ago. Small, inexpensive Fiat cars were the first cars many Italian families could afford to own. Today, Fiat is Europe's most important motor vehicle manufacturer and it produces more than one million cars every year. Fiat factories in Turin and southern Italy also make tractors, trucks and buses. Factories in other countries, including the USSR, are licenced to manufacture Fiat cars. Olivetti, a leading developer and manufacturer of computers and business machines has its offices in Ivrea, near Turin.

Milan is Italy's most important commercial and financial centre. Big banks, insurance companies,

One of Italy's hi-tech industries is the design and manufacture of computers and business machines. These computer circuits are being checked at the Olivetti factory in Ivrea, near Turin.

corporate headquarters and the country's chief stock exchange are housed in the city's fine old buildings and modern office blocks. The city is at the heart of an industrial zone packed with factories of all sizes. There are steel mills and chemical plants, the Pirelli tyre plant and the Alfa Romeo motor vehicle factory. Smaller industries produce an amazing variety of goods. Smothered by fog, industrial smoke and car fumes, Milan has the worst air pollution problem of all of Italy's major cities. Milan, with Rome and Florence, dominates the fashion industry, which is one of Italy's chief sources of income. Although the most exclusive high fashion shows are staged in Rome, most designers and manufacturers of Italian ready-to-wear styles work in Milan. Journalists

Fashion is big business in Italy, where famous designers such as Valentino and Armani thrive. However, the foundation of the fashion world is made up of many small businesses that make clothing and accessories and can adapt quickly to fashion's latest trends.

and buyers from all over the world travel to Milan several times a year to attend specialized fashion shows.

The third city of the industrial triangle is Genoa, which is one of Italy's major ports. Although Genoa has steel mills and chemical plants, it is important mainly as a port of entry for the raw materials for the industries of northern Italy. Although it is some distance from the industrial triangle, Rome is emerging as a major pole of light industry and as a centre of computer technology.

Tinned tomatoes and textiles

Food products are among Italy's leading exports. Olive oil and wine are at the head of the list, with fresh fruit and vegetables not far behind. However, tinned tomatoes and tomato paste, together with preserved fruit, fruit juice and marmalade, rival wine as a major source of income from exports.

The textile industry, which produces silk, cotton, wool and synthetic fabrics, is highly developed in northern and central Italy. Como, near Milan, produces luxurious silks and Prato, near Florence, makes yarns and fabrics for Italy's clothing manufacturers. In many small but prosperous cities in Lombardy and Emilia-Romagna, the sound of knitting machines never ceases. Family-operated businesses turn out huge quantities of knitwear in their own homes, much of it for export. Italian leather goods are famous for style and workmanship. Small industries in central Italy produce shoes, another major export.

Glass, gold and ceramics
Traditions of good craftwork go back centuries and are still practised in the regions today. Glassware has been a speciality of Venice for 1000 years, for example. Venetian glassblowers knew the secret of making clear, colourless glass, a skill that had died out with the ancient Romans. In order to keep others from learning this skill, Venetian glassblowers were forbidden to leave the city or to teach their secrets to outsiders. Today, Venice's glass factories still produce great quantities of glass, from expensive artistic pieces and reproductions of antique glass to modern light fittings and gaudy souvenir gondolas.

Vicenza in the Veneto region, Valenza Po in Piedmont and Arezzo in Tuscany are major

The vehicle manufacturing industry is one of Italy's main sources of export income. The Italian flair for design shows in neat, compact Fiats off the assembly line and in sleek, exclusive sports cars like Ferrari and Maserati.

centres of goldworking. Gold, silver and platinum jewellery is one of Italy's principal exports. The tradition of artistry in gold can be traced back to the ancient Etruscans, who were masters of intricate decoration. Gold earrings and brooches found in Etruscan tombs serve as models for today's goldsmiths.

Ceramics is another ancient art still practised today. Italy's craftworkers produce artistic pottery in both modern and traditional forms, and famous designers sign their names to ceramic tiles used in home decoration. During the Renaissance, the town of Faenza in Emilia-Romagna became famous for beautifully decorated ceramics. The type of ceramics, a glazed-coloured pottery, produced in Faenza is known throughout Europe as *faience*.

Foreign trade and industry abroad

Italy does business with the world, trading goods not only with its partners in the EC but also with far-off countries, such as Japan and Australia. However, Italy's major trading partners are West Germany and France, followed by the United States and the United Kingdom. Italy dominates foreign markets for many different goods, including picture frames, expensive sports cars and some highly-specialized machines for manufacturing.

Industrial development in southern Italy

Southern Italy has little fertile farmland and few sources of power. It also often suffers from drought. For many centuries, it was oppressed by foreign rulers who did little to improve the people's way of life. The south was cut off from the progress that brought prosperity to northern Italy. In order to improve conditions in southern Italy the government set up a special fund for the south, the *Cassa per il Mezzogiorno*, in 1950. The fund financed development of agriculture, transportation and industry in southern Italy and in other regions, such as Abruzzo and Sardinia that share the south's problems. Dams were built in the mountains to provide water. Irrigation systems carried water to parched fields. Water was piped into some towns for the first time and people no longer had to draw water from wells. Northern industries were encouraged to build factories in the south. Unfortunately, some of the south's new industries were steelworks and oil refineries which created new jobs for local workers but also caused pollution. The motorway from the north was continued all the way to the toe of the boot at Reggio Calabria and airports and ports were built.

The fund's investments have not solved all of southern Italy's problems and they have created new ones, such as pollution that keeps tourists away from certain areas. Some of the government money that poured into the south was channelled illegally into the pockets of the Mafia, the criminal organization that arose in Sicily. The Mafia spread to the mainland of Italy and to other parts of the world, mainly the USA. The Camorra, a similar criminal society active in the Campania region, also managed to get hold of funds destined for development. Disastrous earthquakes have worsened overcrowded and inadequate housing conditions, especially in the city of Naples. All these problems mean that the south is still a long way behind the north in terms of wealth and standards of living.

7 Transport and communication

A journey from one end of Italy to the other can be a long one. It takes about 17 hours on an express train to get from Turin in the north to Reggio Calabria on the toe of the boot, and three hours more to get from Reggio Calabria to Palermo in Sicily. By plane, the same trip would take less than two hours. Planes are the fastest way to travel between north and south in Italy. No airport on the mainland or on the main islands is more than one hour away from Rome by plane.

In the days of the Roman empire, people sailed from one port to another along Italy's shores in order to avoid long, difficult journeys over hilly and mountainous land. However, sea voyages could be long and dangerous. About 2000 years ago, the Romans began to build a far-reaching system of roads in order to provide fast, safe routes for messengers, soldiers and merchants. The Romans were able engineers who laid out their roads along the straightest routes possible. They also made their roads fit to last. The Appian Way in Rome for example, was built in 312BC and is still in use.

Motorways
Today, Italy has built another fine system of roads. The network of motorways that stretches to every part of the country is one of the best in Europe. The Autostrada del Sole, Motorway of the Sun, was the country's first major motorway.

The valleys of the Alps provide routes from Italy to other European countries. Superbly-engineered roads climb the mountains, passing through long tunnels through the mountains, and over dams like this one at Lake Gallo on the Swiss frontier.

It connects Milan in the north with Reggio Calabria in the south, covering a distance of 1250 kilometres (750 miles). It has contributed to the development of southern Italy by providing a direct link with the north. Fruit, vegetables and other goods from Sicily can be transported by lorry and arrive in Milan's markets the next day. More than 6000 kilometres (3600 miles) of motorways provide good, fast routes throughout Italy and pass through magnificent scenery most of the way. Italy's network of motorways is the world's largest system after those of the USA and West Germany.

Lorry traffic is heavy on the motorways, carrying almost 75 per cent of all the goods transported in Italy. Most of the motorways are toll roads on which drivers are charged according to the size of their vehicles and the distance they travel. Some of the money collected in tolls is used to improve the motorways.

Tourists from northern Europe drive into Italy over the twisting roads of the Alps. They arrive through long tunnels that pierce the high mountains. The Monte Bianco and Fréjus tunnels between France and Italy are more than 11 kilometres (7 miles) long. In the Apennines, a 10 kilometres (6 mile) tunnel bores through the Gran Sasso mountain. There are more than 22 million motor vehicles on Italy's roads today. Some are trucks and commercial vehicles, but 20 million are motor cars. There is one motor car for every three people living in Italy today. Since 66 per cent of Italians live in cities or towns, the number of vehicles in the urban areas often causes critical problems of traffic congestion and air pollution.

Rome, like many Italian cities, has traffic jams during the rush hour. This not only makes moving around difficult but also pollutes the air. A lot of young people ride motorbikes to dodge among the cars.

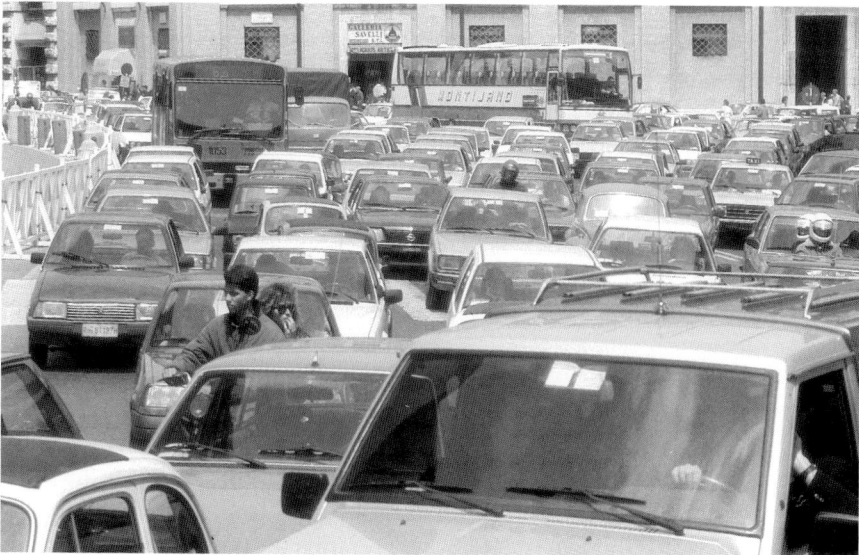

The narrow streets of historic old cities are not suited to traffic. Exhaust fumes poison the air and deposit grime on ancient monuments, causing the stone to crumble.

Travel by rail and by air

Half of Italy's 20 000 kilometres (12 400 miles) of rail lines are electrified. Fast Intercity trains link major cities and Eurocity trains connect Italy with 14 European countries. Many people travel by train. Although carriages are usually comfortable, they may be crowded. Wise travellers reserve their seats in advance. Most long-distance trains have restaurant cars or a self-service buffet car where passengers can get something to eat or drink during the journey.

Travelling by air is also very popular. Alitalia is Italy's national airline. It is state-owned and it flies all over the world. Italy's colours of green, white and red are painted on the tail sections of all Alitalia planes, making them easy to recognize. Italy has a few smaller airlines, some of which are controlled by Alitalia. They fly to many cities in Italy and to offshore islands. About 13 million passengers a year pass though Leonardo da Vinci Airport in Rome. Most people call the airport Fiumicino, which is the name of the city suburb next to the airport.

Ports

Italy has several major ports such as Genoa, Trieste, Venice, Naples, Leghorn and La Spezia. The largest number of passenger ships dock at Naples. Ferries sail from Naples for the islands of Capri and Ischia. Genoa is Italy's most important cargo port. Cargo ships also dock at Trieste, Livorno and Venice, where some tourists are surprised to see large cargo ships sailing down a broad channel within sight of St Mark's Square. Tankers deliver great quantities of crude oil to the ports of Taranto and Augusta in southern Italy, where there are large refineries. Ferries for Yugoslavia and Greece leave from Ancona and Brindisi on Italy's Adriatic coast. Large ferries from the mainland take at least eight hours to reach Sardinia, but ferries can cross the Strait of Messina between Calabria and Sicily in less than half an hour. Ferries connect all of Italy's smaller islands with the mainland. On the large Alpine lakes, ferries carry people and cars from one lake resort to another and provide good views of the scenery.

Palermo in Sicily is situated on a large bay with a deep harbour. In the busy port is a shipbuilding industry and ferries sailing between Sicily and the mainland. Italian ports load and unload about 350 million tonnes (344 million tons) of cargo a year.

Communications

Counting public and office telephones, there is one telephone in Italy for every two people. Although private industries make Italy a leading producer of communications technology, Italians complain that state-owned telephone and postal services are not up to average European standards.

Italians who live in major cities can choose from as many as 30 television channels. There are three state-owned channels, a few privately-owned national channels and numerous local television stations. People who own television sets must pay a yearly tax to help support the state-owned channels. All other channels are financed by advertising.

A few major newspapers and many local newspapers are published in Italy. The daily newspapers *La Repubblica* and *Corriere della Sera* are distributed throughout the country and have the most readers. However, Italians buy fewer newspapers than readers in many other countries. Magazines have about as many readers as newspapers, and there are magazines on a wide range of subjects. In the last 20 years the numbers of Italians who read books has almost tripled. Today, about 75 per cent of the people in Italy regularly read newspapers, magazines or books.

8 Rome and religion

Vatican City in Rome is the world capital of the Roman Catholic Church, headed by the pope. Rome played an important part in the history of the Catholic Church. Jesus Christ's disciples lived in Judea which was then part of the Roman empire. The disciples spread the Christian message throughout the Mediterranean world, and to far distant parts of the Roman empire. The new religion was tolerated by some emperors and persecuted by others. Christ's disciples, Peter and Paul, were killed in Rome for their faith and became Christian martyrs. Peter had been chosen by Christ as the man who was to become the foundation of the Christian Church.

In Rome, early Christians buried their dead in underground cemeteries called catacombs and gathered there to pray. St Peter's body was buried in Rome, and early Christians built a church over his grave. Many centuries later, St Peter's Basilica was built on the same site, in the Vatican.

Most Italians are baptized Roman Catholics, and many of the important events in their lives are marked by a religious ceremony. Six out of ten children make their First Communion. Most weddings are performed in church and people enjoy taking part in religious festivals. However, less than 20 per cent of the Italians attend church regularly. Divorce became legal in 1974, but it is not accepted under Catholicism.

Every town and village in Italy has its own Catholic church, which usually bears the name of the town's patron saint. There are many churches

The First Communion is a very important event in the life of a young Italian. The First Communicants dress up in special clothes, much like those worn by brides and bridegrooms. To mark the occasion relatives and friends are given little packets of sugar-coated almonds called confetti.

in the cities, including a main church or cathedral. The countryside is dotted with monasteries and convents, many of which are empty because fewer people are becoming monks and nuns. Many church buildings in Italy are very old and contain precious works of art. The most splendid church of all is St Peter's Basilica in Vatican City.

Vatican City

Vatican City is the headquarters of the Roman Catholic Church. It is the smallest independent state in the world, with an area of 0.44 kilometres (0.17 square miles). In 1871, Rome had become the official capital of the newly-united Italy but the pope had refused to recognize the new state. Since the fourteenth century the Vatican has been the residence of the popes. Earlier, the popes lived in the Lateran palace next to the basilica of St John Lateran. Although the pope had been allowed to continue to rule over the Vatican, it was only in 1929, when representatives of Pope Pius XI and Mussolini, the Italian leader, signed a treaty, that the Vatican became a separate state.

The Italians often visit shrines devoted to particular saints. The grotto of Saint Rosaria attracts many people with illnesses, as prayers to the saint are thought to help cure them. Tokens representing their ailments are often left behind after the visit.

Inside Vatican City's thick walls are churches, palaces, a magnificent museum and historic library, gardens, office buildings and blocks of flats. The Vatican has its own postal service and issues stamps that are prized by collectors. Vatican City has its own daily newspaper and a radio station that broadcasts in 35 languages. About 700 people live inside this tiny state, which has shops, a supermarket and a petrol station.

The pope

Pope John Paul II is the 264th pope of the Roman Catholic church. The pope is also bishop of Rome. He lives in the Vatican when he is not travelling or at his country residence in Castelgandolfo, overlooking Lake Albano near Rome.

Pope John Paul II is head of the Roman Catholic Church and ruler of Vatican City. He became pope in 1978, when he succeeded Pope John Paul I, who died only 34 days after his election. John Paul II was born in Poland and is the first non-Italian pope to have been elected in 450 years. He has travelled more than any pope, making visits to Roman Catholics in countries all over the world.

To make it easier for him to get about, a helicopter pad was built in the Vatican gardens.

The pope appears in public at the general audiences he holds every week either in St Peter's Square in fair weather, or in a special audience hall inside the Vatican during the cold months. He also appears at noon every Sunday at the window of his study in the Vatican Palace overlooking St Peter's Square. As many as 40 000 people may crowd into the vast square. In 1981, an assassin in the crowd attempted to kill Pope John Paul II.

The Vatican's art treasures
The pope's apartment in the Vatican Palace occupies only a small part of the building, which also contains the Sistine Chapel, where the popes are elected. In 1508, Pope Julius II hired Michelangelo to paint the ceiling of the Sistine Chapel. In order to do so the artist had to learn the fresco method of painting very quickly on wet plaster. He worked on the ceiling for four years, covering every part with scenes from the Bible and with classical figures. More than 20 years later another pope called on him to paint the Last Judgment on the wall above the altar. Michelangelo's works in the Sistine Chapel are among the greatest achievements of Renaissance art. Today, an ambitious international restoration project carried out by Vatican experts is nearing completion. Most of Michelangelo's frescoes have been cleaned, showing his amazing use of colour.

More than two million people a year visit the Sistine Chapel and the Vatican Museum's vast art collections and the library. Even larger numbers of tourists and pilgrims visit St Peter's Basilica.

The Vatican houses many art treasures. If you want to see all of them, you have to walk through 7.25 kilometres (4.50 miles) of displays ranging from Egyptian statues to antique papal carriages. Parts of the vast museum, such as the Sistine Chapel, are located in the pope's palace.

This immense church was completed in the seventeenth century after more than 100 years of planning and building. Michelangelo designed the majestic dome, but much of the lavish interior decoration is the work of Bernini. Michelangelo's marble statue of the *Pieta*, the dead Christ in Mary's arms, is only one of the treasures that St Peter's holds.

The Church today

After 2000 years the Roman Catholic Church is still an important element of life in Italy. Parish priests are energetic in their efforts to encourage people to go to church services. Together with volunteer workers, many priests and nuns are active in programmes to help the homeless and to assist immigrants. Many priests have organized highly successful drug rehabilitation programmes.

Although the Roman Catholic religion is the official religion of Italy, people are free to practise other faiths. There have been Jewish communities in Italy for thousands of years. The largest religious minority group is made up of members of various Protestant churches.

Local traditions add drama and colour to religious holidays in Italy. In most towns and villages there will be a procession carrying a picture or statue of a saint. In Holy Week, before Easter, people in some towns act out the story of Christ's death and resurrection.

9 Education, health and welfare

In Italy the state pays for primary and secondary education and for most of the costs of a university education. Most children attend state schools, but some parents send their children to private schools and pay the school fees. Italian children begin school at six years of age and must continue to go to school until they are at least 14. Many attend nursery school between the ages of three and six. One third of them go to private nursery schools.

Primary and middle schools

Primary schools in Italy cover five years. Classes are made up of about 20 pupils and the atmosphere in the classroom is relaxed and informal. The children wear smocks over their clothes. Most of them carry their books to school in knapsacks on their backs. Lessons usually start at 8.30am and end at 12.30pm. There is a mid-morning break for recreation and a snack, which may be fruit or a sandwich that the children bring from home. Many primary schools have full-time programmes offering a school lunch and activities, such as sports and crafts in the afternoon. Most children go to school six days a week, from Monday to Saturday. During the first two years of primary school, children improve their skills in reading, writing and expression and do simple arithmetic. Later on they study history and geography too. There are no report cards, but teachers give parents a written report of their child's progress.

Primary school children leaving school carry bags for their homework. These children will soon be learning a foreign language, thanks to a school reform law passed recently. Most children in the middle school already study English or French as a foreign language.

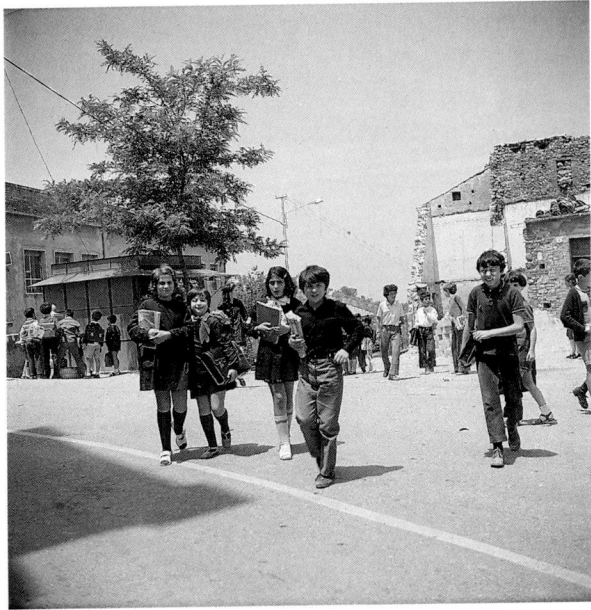

Children usually finish the fifth year when they are 11 and then they start the first of three years of middle school. The school day is slightly longer, with classes until 1.30pm. In middle school, lessons in science and a foreign language are added to the programme. Accompanied by their teachers, children make excursions to see people, places and things that can help them get a better understanding of what they are studying. After school, pupils do their homework and may enjoy watching children's programmes on television or playing sports. Some schools and many Catholic parish churches organize sports activities for the after-school hours.

After three years of middle school or **scuola media,** or at age 14, a child can leave school. A proposal that would raise the age limit for compulsory education is being discussed. However, most children take an exam to gain their middle school diploma and they continue their education.

Secondary schools

When children move to secondary schools, they have a variety of choices including classical, scientific or professional studies. Most of these schools have five year programmes. In secondary school, classes may last from 8 or 8.30am until 1.30 or 2.30pm. Pupils usually spend at least part of the afternoon studying. At the end of the final year of secondary school, they must take a series of exams in order to earn their diploma. In most cases the diploma entitles the pupil to attend a

Secondary schools are often in old buildings in the centre of towns, like this school in the Via Martelli in Florence. Many of the pupils arrive by motorbike.

university. Pupils who have gone to vocational or some other types of schools must pass an additional exam in order to enrol at a university.

The calendar of the school year varies from one region to another. Children start the school year later in the south, where summers are long and very hot. In central Italy pupils in primary, middle and secondary schools attend lessons from mid-September to mid-June. The Christmas holiday last about two weeks and Easter holidays are about ten days. There are many one-day holidays, too. In the spring, pupils may join class trips to some of Italy's most interesting and historic places.

Universities

More than a million students are enrolled in Italy's universities. University courses last from four to six years, and students must take a large number of exams. They also must write a thesis, or essay, and discuss it before a board of professors in order to earn a degree. Most of the universities are state universities. Students pay fees of about 200 000 lire each year.

Italy has some of Europe's oldest universities. The University of Bologna was founded 900 years ago and is famous for its schools of medicine and law. Many of Italy's 25 state universities were in existence in the thirteenth and fourteenth centuries. Classes may still be held in historic buildings.

Health care and pensions

Taxes collected by the government pay for Italy's national health service, which provides health care

Lectures at universities are usually very crowded. This university at Cosenza in Calabria has about 6000 students, but the largest universities have well over 100 000 students each.

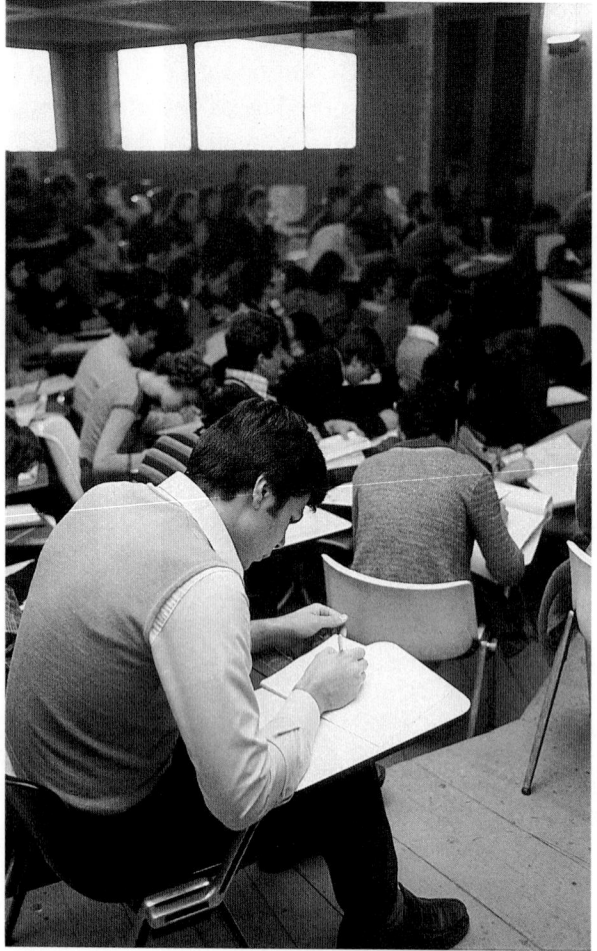

for most citizens. Each family has a family doctor who can authorize laboratory tests and request that his patients be visited by medical specialists if necessary. Families with small children also have a specialist children's doctor. Children must have all the required vaccinations before they can start school. Hospital care is guaranteed in public hospitals. There are many private hospitals where patients pay fees for care. The national health service is supervised by a government office in Rome but is organized at local levels. This accounts for some differences in the quality of care.

Some of Italy's hospitals are very old. In Rome the hospital of San Giovanni has existed since the thirteenth century when it was founded to care for pilgrims to the church of Saint John Lateran. The hospital of the Santo Spirito, or Holy Spirit, in Rome was built by a fifteenth century pope as a place of rest and cure for pilgrims to Saint Peter's.

Like many Europeans, Italians believe in the healing properties of hot springs, mineral waters and radioactive mud and vapours, all of which are available at Italy's spas. Many people spend a week or two every year taking treatments at one of the spas. The most fashionable and elegant spas are Montecatini and Salsomaggiore in central Italy.

A system of social security run by the state pays pensions to retired and elderly people. As people live longer today, thanks to better health care, old people make up a larger part of Italy's population than ever before. The country faces the problem of finding enough funds to pay their pensions. Men in Italy can expect to live to be 73 years old while women can expect to live to 79. Today, the number of births and number of deaths every year are equal. Although the population is not growing, the Italians are, and the average young Italian adult is about five centimetres (two inches) taller than his parents.

10 Tourism and the arts

More than 20 million foreign tourists visit Italy every year. Some of them are attracted by the country's warm sunny climate and lively holiday resorts. Many want to see Italy's historic cities and glorious art treasures. Almost everyone enjoys the beautiful scenery and good food. Tourism is a major source of income for the country. It provides jobs for many people in hotels, restaurants and other activities related to travel.

More tourists visit Italy during the Easter season than at any other time of year. At Easter, Rome is crowded with people, and many of them attend solemn religious ceremonies in St Peter's Basilica. After Easter, the tourist season continues until early autumn. During the hot summer months, many people from countries in northern Europe enjoy holidays at seaside resorts along the Ligurian or Adriatic coasts. In August, many Italians take their holidays, too. Some tourists prefer to visit Italy during the winter when museums and other places of interest are less crowded.

People from all over the world can be seen tossing a coin into the Fountain of Trevi in Rome, a traditional gesture that is said to ensure their return. Most visitors usually spend a few days in one or all of Italy's three most important cities of Rome, Florence and Venice. There are also tours of the islands of Sicily or Sardinia and of the hill towns of Tuscany and Umbria. Some tours are planned to appeal to people with special interests. Archaeologists may take tours of Etruscan, Greek

Even during the autumn and early spring many cafes are filled with tourists, specially in popular tourist locations like Venice.

or Roman sites that are still being excavated. People who love opera may visit the birthplace of the composer Giuseppe Verdi and attend performances at Milan's famous La Scala opera theatre. People who appreciate good food may take gourmet tours, eating in some of Italy's best restaurants.

Rome

The most popular attraction in Italy is the city of Rome. In Rome visitors can see the classical majesty of Roman ruins and the splendour of St Peter's, or admire Rome's rooftops and church domes from the top of the Spanish Steps, a graceful eighteenth century marble staircase in the heart of the city. Some people like to count the different kinds of stone animals on the city's beautiful fountains. There are bees, turtles, lions, horses, dolphins and many others. They can have an espresso coffee or a *tartufo* (chocolate truffle) ice cream at a pavement cafe, or escape from the noise and confusion of city traffic by strolling under the umbrella pines in Villa Borghese, a peaceful park.

Rome is almost 3000 years old. It is called the Eternal City. The city's long history can be traced by visiting monuments such as the Forum, where Julius Caesar walked, and the Colosseum, where the gladiators fought. Visitors can admire sparkling mosaics in the churches where early Christians prayed. Narrow streets in the oldest districts have changed little during the past 500 years. Lavishly decorated churches and palaces are reminders of the centuries when Rome was the splendid centre of the papal court. The city's museums and churches contain some of the world's finest works of art.

Florence

Florence is the city of the Medicis and the artistic treasures that this wealthy family collected. There are many remarkable sights in Florence. The huge tapered dome of the cathedral and the dark stone Palazzo Vecchio, Old Palace, were built about 450 years ago, soon after the Medicis came to power. Michelangelo's towering statue of David and the statues on the Medici family tombs are among the Florentine artist's most powerful works. The bridge called the Ponte Vecchio, Old Bridge, was built across the Arno River in 1345. It is lined with shops displaying the wares of goldsmiths and silversmiths. Ponte Vecchio survived a disastrous flood in 1966 that damaged many of Florence's buildings.

Among the sights that attract thousands of visitors to Rome each year are the Roman ruins of the Forum and monuments such as the triumphal arch of the Emperor Titus. Triumphal arches were built by the Romans to celebrate victories or to honour emperors. This arch was erected to celebrate the capture of Jerusalem in AD70 by Emperor Titus.

Venice

The fabulous city of Venice was built on water 1000 years ago. It was founded by people who settled on a cluster of mud banks and marshy islands in the middle of a shallow lagoon in the northern Adriatic Sea. The settlers drove logs deep into the mud to make foundations for their houses and churches. The settlement grew into a unique and beautiful city that became a mighty sea power and an enormously wealthy state. To get about in Venice people must walk or take a boat. Water-buses called *vaporetti* transport people along the Grand Canal and circle the city. Only small boats and gondolas, typical Venetian craft, can pass through most of Venice's 159 canals. More than 400 little bridges cross the canals,

Venice attracts so many tourists that occasionally they outnumber the city's 80 000 residents. Tourists flock to St Mark's Square or to the Rialto bridge. They enjoy riding on the gondolas moored along the banks of the Grand Canal. The gondoliers who steer these boats wear traditional costume.

connecting narrow, crooked streets.

Venice has numerous churches, large and small, and beautiful palaces that were built many centuries ago. Venice's largest and finest church, St Mark's Basilica, gleams with golden mosaics and rich marble. Some palaces look crooked because portions of their foundations are sinking

Gondolas

Gondolas are Venice's most famous boats. They have an elegant traditional form and must be painted black. Until the sixteenth century, Venetian nobles painted their family gondolas in many colours, covering them with lavish decorations. The state disapproved, and in 1562 it decreed that gondolas had to be black. Gondolas are rowed by gondoliers, who use a single oar set into a beautifully carved wooden oarlock that is notched so that the gondolier can change the oar's position rapidly.

deeper into the mud. Venice has its own fire boats, ambulance boats, police and postal boats.

Places worth a visit

Italy has many smaller cities that are worth visiting. Pisa in Tuscany has the famous Leaning Tower, which is really the bell tower of the cathedral. The tower began to tilt to one side soon after it was built 800 years ago, and it leans about one more millimetre each year. Today, it leans about 4.5 metres (14 feet). Siena, also in Tuscany, has preserved the appearance of a prosperous town of the twelfth and thirteenth century, with fine buildings in red brick and a magnificent marble cathedral. In southern Italy, people can see the majestic Greek temples of Paestum, near Naples, and of Agrigento, in Sicily. Ravenna in the northeast and Monreale near Palermo are famous for beautiful mosaics, some of them 1000 years old.

The Leaning Tower of Pisa is the most famous of the group of buildings that include Pisa's cathedral and baptistry, all in the rich Pisan style of architecture.

People go to the Alpine lakes or to the Amalfi Coast near Naples to enjoy stunning scenery.

The arts in Italy

The Italians have a genius for art. For thousands of years up to the present, artists, authors, musicians and craftworkers have made Italy a centre of achievement in all the arts. Etruscan and Roman art fill some of Italy's most important museums. Churches all over Italy contain the works of great artists of all ages, such as Giotto, Raphael, Michelangelo, Bernini and Titian. Modern art galleries show paintings by the twentieth century masters Modigliani, De Chirico and sculptor Manzu.

Italian literature was inspired by the classical works of Latin poets, such as Virgil and Horace. The language of literature developed from the thirteenth century works of Dante, Petrarch and Boccaccio.

The story of the puppet Pinocchio is a favourite of children all over the world. It was written by Carlo Collodi in the 1880s. Today, puppet shows are still a popular entertainment in Sicily. Italians invented the form of theatre known as the *Commedia dell' Arte,* with masked actors improvising dialogue to entertain the audience. Italian author Luigi Pirandello is one of the major playwrights of the twentieth century. Other popular authors of the twentieth century include Ignazio Silone, who wrote about life in the undeveloped south, and Italo Calvino, whose numerous fables have won acclaim.

Many Italians enjoy listening to music, especially opera. In the seventeenth century, the

Italians invented opera in the 1500s and they are still enthusiastic fans of this mixture of music and theatre. During the cooler months they enjoy performances of operas by Verdi, Puccini and others in theatres such as La Scala in Milan. In the summer they fill the vast spaces of Verona's Roman Arena or the ruins of Pompeii to hear opera in the open air.

first opera was written by composer Claudio Monteverdi to entertain the duke of Mantua and his court. Opera became very popular in the nineteenth century, when Guiseppe Verdi wrote such works as *Aida* and *La Traviata*. Another leading composer, Giacomo Puccini wrote *Tosca* and *Madame Butterfly*.

The cinema

Today, the cinema is an important art form in Italy. During the 1950s and 1960s so many major films were made in Rome's cinema centre, Cinecittà, that Rome was called Hollywood-on-the-Tiber. Italy's scenery and climate are ideal for shooting films, but it is the new methods and ideas introduced by Italian filmmakers which are most impressive.

11 Eating in Italy

Food is important in the Italian way of life but Italian cooking is quite simple. Its success depends on the freshness and quality of the ingredients. Many dishes are prepared and cooked just before they are served, with their taste and aroma at a peak. Italians in general like to eat well. The average Italian family spends more on food than on any other item in the family budget. Italians may be willing to spend more to buy the best ingredients, but they know how to be thrifty if necessary. They take great pride in their cooking and make special efforts to serve their guests the best food possible.

Markets and shops
Many people go to market every weekday morning in order to have the freshest ingredients for their meals. If they are having guests to dinner they tell stallholders so. The stallholders know that in this case, they must give their customers only the best. Italian markets are lively and colourful. They are usually held outdoors in city squares. Markets are open every weekday morning in large cities. In small towns they may be held once or twice a week. The stallholders arrive in the marketplace at dawn, set up their stalls and pile them high with fruits and vegetables of all kinds. Before long people come to choose from mounds of bright oranges and shiny apples. They pick over heaps of leafy broccoli and pyramids of plump tomatoes. Stalls decorated with fern fronds and sliced lemons display a great variety of fish.

Italians prefer fresh ingredients to pre-packaged convenience foods. Many like to choose their fruit and vegetables at outdoor markets where they can bargain over prices and exchange good-natured remarks with the vendors.

White-coated stallholders sell meat and poultry. Above the counter long ropes of sausages are draped like ribbons. There are also stalls selling cheese, dairy products, hams and salami. There is usually a flower stall at the market, and there may be stalls selling kitchen utensils or even clothing. By early afternoon whatever hasn't been sold has been packed up and carted away to storage until the next market day. The stalls are dismantled and heaps of discarded fruit and vegetables swept into garbage bins. Workers with hoses wash the pavement and the market place once again looks like an ordinary square.

Some people find it more convenient to shop at the supermarkets that can be found in most cities and towns in Italy. Markets are open only in the

Prosciutto, raw cured ham, is one of Italy's most famous food specialities. Prosciutto is produced in many regions, but that from the area around Parma is known for its sweet, nutlike flavour. Italians like to eat prosciutto with fresh mozzarella cheese, with slices of cold melon or with fresh figs.

morning while supermarkets and food shops are open both morning and afternoon. Like all other shops, they may close for a long lunch hour, but they remain open until around 7.30pm. Food shops called *alimentari* may sell almost as many types of products as a supermarket, though quantities are limited. In an alimentari shop people may find everything from cheese and salami to shampoo and detergents. Some food shops are highly specialized, such as a *macelleria* (butcher shop) or a *frutteria* (greengrocer).

Pasta

Pasta is probably the best known Italian food speciality and it is a staple of the Italian diet. In central and southern Italy, pasta is an essential part of the meal. Pasta is made of durum wheat flour and water. In the north, however, people may eat *risotto*, creamy rice, or *polenta*, boiled corn meal served with rich sauce, instead of pasta as a first course. Butter is widely used in northern Italian cooking, and olive oil is used in central and southern Italy.

Fresh eggs may be blended with the flour to make egg pasta. Finely chopped spinach may be added to make green pasta, a speciality of Bologna. Pasta must be cooked in a deep pot full of boiling, salted water. Italians like their pasta *al dente*, chewy, and they are very careful not to overcook it.

Pasta comes in countless varieties and is served with all kinds of sauces. Each region and many towns have local types of pasta that may be known by a name in dialect. Often, a particular type of

The Etruscans left evidence that pasta was eaten in Italy as early as the sixth century BC. Stone carvings in an Etruscan tomb in Cerveteri near Rome show a rolling pin and board for rolling out fresh pasta and the small wheeled instrument used to cut it. This freshly made pasta is about to be cut into one of the many different shapes in which it is served.

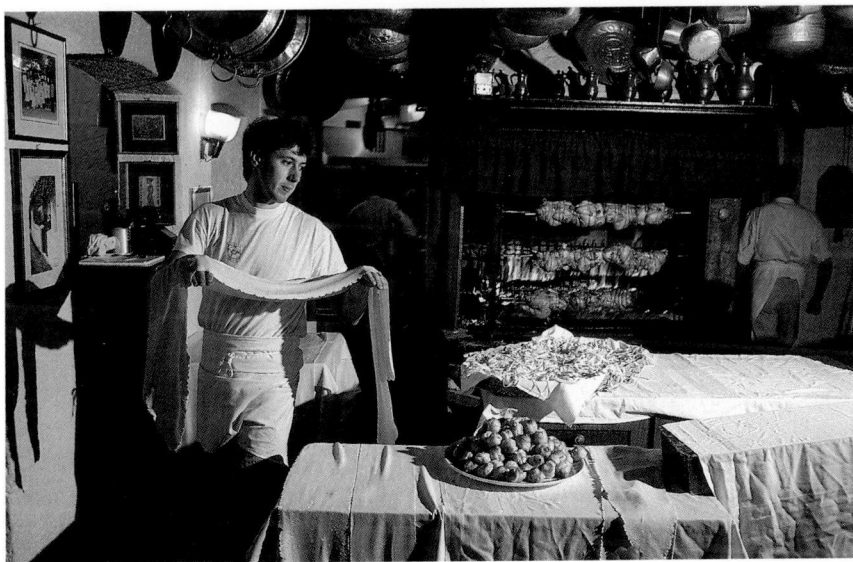

pasta is served on a particular occasion. In Naples, *lasagne* is always served at Christmas and Easter. Standard types of pasta are sold in packages in shops. Freshly made egg pasta can be bought in specialist shops. Each type of pasta is named according to its shape. Even babies eat tiny forms of pasta called *pastina*. Stuffed pasta requires extra preparation. Like lasagne, it was traditionally served only on Sundays and special occasions, but today it can be found at any meal. All of the stuffed pastas are usually served with a savoury sauce. They are good, too, with melted butter and a sprinkling of grated Parmesan cheese. The best Parmesan cheese is made in the Emilia-Romagna region in huge round forms weighing at least 24 kilograms (52 pounds).

There is a great variety of Italian cheese ranging from the creamy Dolcelatte to the very hard Parmesan, seen hanging in these large round balls. Parmesan is usually served finely grated, with pasta dishes.

Meals

Meal times vary from north to south. In central Italy lunch may begin at 1 or 1.30pm. People usually have supper at 8 or 8.30pm. Meal times are a little earlier in the north and a little later in the south. An everyday main meal begins with a first course of pasta or a thick soup, such as *minestrone*, a vegetable soup with little tubes of pasta cooked in it. A second course of meat or fish is usually served with a vegetable or salad. People may eat fruit for dessert. At Sunday dinner or on special occasions an *antipasto*, or starter, may be served before the pasta course. A traditional antipasto is made up of thin slices of prosciutto, parma ham, and salami with some pickled vegetables and olives. Prosciutto may also be served with fresh figs or chilled melon. There may be two second courses at a special dinner, and there is always a dessert. For many centuries, sweet dishes were served throughout the meal. The menu of a dinner at the court of the dukes of Ferrara in the sixteenth century lists an 'antipasto' of marmalade, marzipan, which is an almond paste, and small pastries. By the nineteenth century, desserts were served at the end of the meal, although people ate fruit ices between courses to refresh their sense of taste. Today, Italian pastry shops are especially busy on Sunday, when people buy pastries for dessert at family dinners. *Gelato*, ice-cream, is an Italian invention and there are *gelati* shops everywhere in Italy.

People drink mineral water or wine with their meals, and children may drink water with a little wine added. There are almost as many types of mineral water as there are types of wine in Italy.

Changing habits

The eating habits of many Italians are changing. People who work in offices may have little time for lunch. At midday they may eat at a fast food shop or snack bar. Families may have their main meal together in the evening, and it is usually lighter than the traditional midday meal. For a light supper people often go to a pizzeria, a simple eating place that serves pizza made in white-hot wood-burning ovens. Pizza was invented in Naples. Pizza makers have created numerous variations, but the classic pizza is Neapolitan pizza. It is made of dough, red tomato pulp and creamy mozzarella cheese.

Pizza, pasta, ice cream and espresso coffee all came from Italy and are popular around the world. However, today people in other countries are becoming familiar with many other Italian dishes and ingredients. Elegant Italian restaurants abroad and articles in glossy foreign magazines are making Italian food fashionable. Doctors say that many Italian foods, such as olive oil, are good for you. People are interested in finding out how the Italians cook so that they can make their own Italian dishes. Many Italian food products can be found in supermarkets and specialist shops throughout the world. Food products are among Italy's most important exports. The culture of Italy has widely influenced eating habits in North America, Australia and other European countries as well as making its mark in the arts, fashion and industry.

Index